ARMOR BEARER'S PRAYERS TO GOD

DR. TAVANE GLASS

The opinions expressed in this manuscript are solely the opinions of the author and do not represent the opinions or thoughts of the publisher. The author has represented and warranted full ownership and/or legal right to publish all the materials in this book.

Armor Bearer's Prayers to God
All Rights Reserved.
Copyright © 2016 Dr. Tavane Glass
v2.0

Cover Photo © 2016 thinkstockphotos.com. All rights reserved - used with permission.

Scriptures. Quotations taken from the New International Version (NIV), Copyright 2001 by Crossway,
    a publishing ministry of Good News Publishers.
Scriptures. Quotations taken from the English Standard Version (ESV). Copyright 1982 by Thomas Nelson, Inc.
Scriptures. Quotations taken from the English Standard Version (ESV). Copyright 1982 by Thomas Nelson, Inc.
Scriptures. Quotations taken from the King James Version (KJV). Public domain
Scriptures. Quotations taken from the New Living Translation (NLT). Copyright 1996, 2004, 2007 by Tyndale
    House foundation. Used by permission of Tyndale House Publishers, Inc. Carol Stream Illinois 60188.
Scriptures. Quotations taken from the Amplified Bible (AMB). Copyright 1954, 1958, 1962, 1964, 1965, 1987
    by The Lock man Foundation.
Scriptures. Quotations taken from the New American Standard (NAS). Copyright 1960, 1962, 1963, 1968,
    1971, 1972, 1973, 1975, 1995 by The Lock man Foundation Used by permission www.lockman.org.

This book may not be reproduced, transmitted, or stored in whole or in part by any means, including graphic, electronic, or mechanical without the express written consent of the publisher except in the case of brief quotations embodied in critical articles and reviews.

Outskirts Press, Inc.
http://www.outskirtspress.com

ISBN: 978-1-4787-6956-9

Outskirts Press and the "OP" logo are trademarks belonging to Outskirts Press, Inc.

PRINTED IN THE UNITED STATES OF AMERICA

Dedication

I would like to dedicate this book to my Heavenly Father, the Lord Jesus Christ, whom I adore. I thank you Lord, for allowing me to share your Word with all the armor bearers and servants of God. All Glory and Honor belongs to you. Also, I would like to thank you for letting this book be a blessing to the Kingdom of God.

Foreword

Tavane Glass is a rare jewel—a combination of many gifts, skills, training and anointing. She possesses a deep love and devotion for God. She's been my friend for nearly two decades and for as long as I have known her; she has consistently demonstrated her greatest gift through serving others.

The word of God states; "Do nothing from selfishness or empty conceit, but with humility of mind regard one another as more important than yourselves; do not merely look out for your own personal interests, but also for the interests of others" (Philippians 2:3–4)

Servant hood is Tavane's calling and passion. She exhibits the qualities of a faithful servant. Her latest book is an accumulation of years of lessons learned through serving and life. In addition, the content of her book is powerful and inspiring. Everyone who reads it will be encouraged and compelled to serve others more selflessly.

Serving as an Area Ministry Leader and Staff Pastor's wife, I can say this new book…………..is one that I highly recommend.

Joyce B. Linyear

Acknowledgements

Pastor Janeen McBath
I would like to thank you for giving me the opportunity to be a part of your leadership class. I was truly blessed by being a part of your class. It has equipped me and prepared me for my assignment as an armor bearer. I'm very grateful for your teachings. May God continue to bless you as you continue to be a blessing to the body of Christ.

Spiritual Leader
I would like to thank you for giving me the opportunity to serve you. My experience as your personal assistant will be a part of my life forever. I appreciate everything you have imparted in me. I love you, and may God bless you indeed.

Introduction

One day while sitting in my prayer room, it was revealed to me from my Heavenly Father to write this book. After writing my first book, "Effective Tools on How to become a Successful Armor Bearer and Servant of God," I had no idea God would have me to write my second book the following year, but God knows all things. When God gives you an assignment, it's not debatable, it's a command. God has destined a path for us to travel, and we should travel it without hesitation. Therefore, we should be obedient to God's will for our life because in the end, God will get the glory and others will be blessed for our obedience.

God called me to be an armor bearer for a woman of God, and I served as her personal assistant for four in a half years. I prayed every day for her. Therefore, it is important for armor bearers and servants of God to pray without ceasing. As God's chosen vessels, we are to stand in the gap and pray for our leaders and be their intercessors. Also, it's important for servants to pray for themselves.

In the Bible, God allowed the devil to attack Job, and God allows the enemy through people to attack us. Servant hood is like being enlisted in the army. For instance, soldiers are equipped and armored for battle because their enemies are ready to attack at all times, and servants are constantly being attack by their enemies. Soldiers are trained to attack their enemies in battle. They go through intense training to prepare themselves for battle.

Therefore, we should learn from the soldiers, and prepare ourselves for battle because the enemy "prowls around like a roaring lion, looking for someone to devour". (1st Peter 5:8) We are on the battle field for the Lord, and we should stay in position. We are in spiritual warfare because of our assignments. When you serve your leaders and carry their burdens the enemy is angry. In Hebrews chapter 13:3 it states, "I will never leave you nor forsake you."

At times, it may seem as though your assignment is too much for you to handle. However, God will not put more on you than you can bear. When you feel overwhelmed, ask God to carry your burdens and place His easy yoke upon you. It's important to have a personal relationship with the Lord. Always remember, to put God first when serving your leaders, read the Bible daily and keep your eyes on the Lord. Therefore, God will lead, guide and direct your path when it comes to serving your leaders.

In this book, I have scriptures from the Word of God for servants and armor bearers to pray. These scriptures will build up your faith when you're experiencing obstacles when serving your leaders. These scriptures will encourage you as you serve your leaders as well as serving in your area of ministry. In addition, these scriptures will help servants of God to pray for their leaders concerning issues they may be going through. This book is an awesome tool for armor bearers and servants of God to have in their possession while serving for the Kingdom of God.

What is an Armor Bearer?

An armor bearer is chosen from God, and a watch man on the wall for their leaders. Armor bearers stand in the gap and pray for their leaders continuously. They shield and protect leaders from their enemies. Also, they battle in the spirit realm for their leaders, and lay down their life for their leaders.

Table of Contents

Anger	1
Anxiety	4
Blessings	8
Boasting	10
Boldness	13
Faithful	16
Favor	19
Fear	21
Forgiveness	25
Fruits of the Spirit	28
God's Chosen	31
Healed	34
Honor	38
Jealousy	40
Judgment	47
Listen	50
Love	53
Lying	57
Mercy	59
Obedience	63
Patience	65
Protection	67
Purpose	72
Righteous	75
Revenge	77
Salvation	80
Suffering	82
Trouble	86
Trust	89
Weakness	91
Wisdom	95

1
Anger

Father in Heaven, I ask you to teach me how to serve from a pure heart and remove all anger and bitterness from me in the name of Jesus, Amen.

ARMOR BEARER'S PRAYERS TO GOD

Powerful Scriptures Armor Bearers and Servants of God can pray Daily

Anger

But for those who are self- seeking and who reject the truth and follow evil, there will be wrath and anger. There will be trouble and distress for every human being who does evil

(Romans 2:8-9NIV)

Do not have anything to do with foolish and stupid discussions, because you know they breed arguments

(2 Timothy 2 verse 23 International Standard Version)

Get rid of all bitterness, rage and anger, brawling and slander, along with every form of malice. Be kind and compassionate to one another, forgiving each other, just as in Christ God forgave you

(Ephesians 4 Verses 31-32 New International Version)

ARMOR BEARER'S PRAYERS TO GOD

Powerful Scriptures
Armor Bearers and Servants of God
can pray Daily

Anger

A fool gives full vent to his anger,[1] but a wise man keeps himself under control.[2]

(Proverbs 29:11 NIV)

for man's anger[1] does not bring about the righteous life that God desires

(James 1:20 NIV)

But now you must rid yourselves[1] of all such things as these: anger, rage, malice, slander,[2] and filthy language from your lips.

(Colossians 3:8 NIV)

A hot-tempered man stirs up dissension,[1] but a patient man calms a quarrel.

(Proverbs 15:18 NIV)

2
Anxiety

*Father in Heaven, remove anxiety from me
so I can serve with a spirit of excellence
in the name of Jesus, Amen.*

ARMOR BEARER'S PRAYERS TO GOD

Powerful Scriptures
Armor Bearers and Servants of God
can pray Daily

Anxiety

*Likewise, ye younger, submit yourselves unto the elder,
Yea all of you be subject one to another, and be clothed with humility:
for God resist the proud, and giveth grace to the humble.*

(1Peter5 Verses 5-6 Standard King James Version)

*Trust in the Lord with all your heart and lean not on your own
understanding; in all your ways acknowledge him,
and he will make your paths straight.*

(Proverbs 3:5-6 NIV)

*Do not be anxious about anything, but in everything by prayer and
petition, with thanksgiving, present your requests to God,
which transcends all your hearts and your minds in Christ Jesus.*

(Philippians 4:6-7 NIV)

ARMOR BEARER'S PRAYERS TO GOD

Powerful Scriptures
Armor Bearers and Servants of God
can pray Daily

Anxiety

Peace I leave with you; my peace I give you. I do not give to you. I do not give to you as the world gives. Do not let your hearts be troubled and do not be afraid.

(John 14:27 NIV)

Now may the Lord of peace himself give you peace at all times and in every way. The Lord be with all of you.

(2 Thessalonians 3:16 NIV)

Cast all your cares on the Lord and he will sustain you; he will never let the righteous fall.

(Psalm 55:22 NIV)

Humble yourselves, therefore, under God's mighty hand, that he may lift you up in due time .Cast all your anxiety on him because he cares for you. Be self-controlled and alert. Your enemy the devil prowls around like a roaring lion looking for someone to devour.

(1Peter 5:6-8 NIV)

Powerful Scriptures Armor Bearers and Servants of God can pray Daily

Anxiety

Even though I walk through the valley of the shadow of death, I will fear no evil, for you are with me; your rod and staff, they comfort me. I will trust in you.

(Psalm 23:4 NIV)

When I am afraid, I will be with you.

(Psalms 56:3 NIV)

Come to me, all you who are weary and burdened, and I will give you rest. Take my yoke upon you and learn from me, for I am gentle and humble in heart, and you will find rest for your souls. For my yoke is easy and my burden is light.

(Matthew 11:28-3 NIV)

3
Blessings

Father in Heaven, bless me indeed to serve for your glory in the name of Jesus I pray, Amen.

ARMOR BEARER'S PRAYERS TO GOD

Powerful Scriptures Armor Bearers and Servants of God can pray Daily

Blessings

May he give you the desires of your heart and make all your plans succeed.

(Psalms 20:4 NIV)

Commit to the Lord whatever you do, and he will establish your plans

(Proverbs 16:3 NIV)

For I know the plans I have for you, declares the Lord, plans to prosper you not to harm you, plans to give you hope and a future.

(Jeremiah 29:11 NIV)

And my God meet all your needs according to the riches of his glory in Christ Jesus.

(Philippians 4:19 NIV)

4
Boasting

Father in Heaven, I pray you will give me a humble spirit in the name of Jesus, Amen.

ARMOR BEARER'S PRAYERS TO GOD

Powerful Scriptures
Armor Bearers and Servants of God
can pray Daily

Boasting

*Taste and see that the Lord is good;
blessed is the one who takes refuge in him.*

(Psalms 34:8 NIV)

But to you who are listening I say: Love your enemies, do good to those who hate you, bless those who curse you, pray for those who mistreat you.

(Luke 6: 27-28 NIV)

*But the fruit of the Spirit is love, joy, peace, forbearance, kindness, goodness, faithfulness, gentleness and self-control.
Against such things there is no law.*

(Galatians 5:22-23 NIV)

Do not repay evil or insult with insult. On the Contrary, repay evil with blessing, because to this you were called so that you may inherit a blessing.

(1 Peter 3:9 NIV)

ARMOR BEARER'S PRAYERS TO GOD

Powerful Scriptures Armor Bearers and Servants of God can pray Daily

Boasting

So don't boast about following a particular human leader. For everything belongs to you

(Corinthians 3:21 New Living Translation)

Do not boast of [yourself and] tomorrow, for you know not what a day may bring forth. Let another man praise you, and not your own month; a stranger, and not your own lips.

(Proverbs 27-1 Amplified Bible (AMP)

For by grace you have been saved through faith. And this is not your own doing; it is the gift of God, not a result of work, so that no one may boast.

(Ephesian 2:8-9 English Standard Version)

"I can do nothing on my own .As I hear, I judge, and my judgment is just, because I seek not my own will but the will of him who sent me."

(John 5:30 English Standard Version)

5
Boldness

Father in Heaven, give me a spirit of boldness as I serve in the name of Jesus I pray, Amen.

ARMOR BEARER'S PRAYERS TO GOD

Powerful Scriptures Armor Bearers and Servants of God can pray Daily

Boldness

See, I have this day appointed you to all the oversight of the nations and of the kingdoms to root out and pull down, to destroy and to overthrow, to build and to plant.

(Jeremiah 1:10 Amplified Bible)

In the day when I called, You answered me; for You strengthened me with strength (might and inflexibility to temptation) in my inner self.

(Psalms 138:3 Amplified Bible)

The wicked flee when no man pursues them, but the uncompromisingly righteous are bold as a lion.

(Proverbs 28:1 Amplified Bible)

And now, Lord, observe their threats and grant to Your bond servants full freedom to declare Your message fearlessly

(Acts 4:29Ampplified Bible)

ARMOR BEARER'S PRAYERS TO GOD

Powerful Scriptures
Armor Bearers and Servants of God
can pray Daily

Boldness

And pray also for me, that [freedom of] utterance may be given me, that I may open my mouth to proclaim boldly the mystery of the good news the Gospel

(Ephesians 6:19 Amplified Bible)

Let us then fearlessly and confidently and boldly draw near to the throne of grace (the throne of God's unmerited favor to us sinners), that we may receive mercy for our failures and find grace to help in good time for every need appropriate help and well-timed help, coming just when we need it.

(Hebrews 4:16 Amplified Bible)

In Whom, because of our faith in Him, we declare to have the boldness courage and confidence of free access an unreserved approach to God with freedom and without fear.

(Ephesians 3:12 Amplified Bible)

6
Faithful

Father in Heaven, help me to be faithful in the assignment you have called me too in the name of Jesus, Amen

Powerful Scriptures Armor Bearers and Servants of God can pray Daily

Faithful

He who is faithful in a very little thing is faithful also in much, and he who is dishonest and unjust in a very little thing is dishonest and unjust also in much.

(Luke 16:10 Amplified Bible)

For God shows no partiality undue favor or unfairness: with Him one man is not different from another.

(Romans 2:11 Amplified Bible)

If you really keep the royal law found in scriptures "Love your neighbors as yourself", you are doing right. But if you show favoritism, you sin and are convicted by the law as law breakers.

(James 2: 8-9 NIV)

"His master replied: Well done, good and faithful servant! You have been faithful with a few things; I will put you in charge of many things, come and share your master's happiness!

(Matthew 25:11 NIV)

ARMOR BEARER'S PRAYERS TO GOD

Powerful Scriptures
Armor Bearers and Servants of God
can pray Daily

Faithful

"So you shall observe to do just as the LORD your God has commanded you; you shall not turn aside to the right or to the left." You shall walk in all the way which the LORD your God has commanded you, that you may live and that it may be well with you, and that you may prolong your days in the land which you will possess

(Deuteronomy 5:32-33 New American Standard Bible)

I thank Christ Jesus our Lord, who has strengthened me, because He considered me faithful, putting me into service

(1 Timothy 1:12 New American Standard Bible)

rejoicing in hope, persevering in tribulation, devoted to prayer

(Romans 12:12 New American Standard Bible)

Therefore, my beloved brethren, be steadfast, immovable, always abounding in the work of the Lord, knowing that your toil is not in vain in the Lord.

(1 Corinthians 15:58 New American Standard Bible)

7
Favor

*Father in Heaven, give me favor with You
and with my leaders in the name of Jesus, Amen.*

ARMOR BEARER'S PRAYERS TO GOD

Powerful Scriptures Armor Bearers and Servants of God can pray Daily

Favor

Joseph found favor in his eyes and became his attendant. Potiphar put him in charge of his household, and he entrusted to his care everything he owned.

(Genesis 39:4 NIV)

And David came to Saul, and stood befre him: and he loved him greatly; and he became his armourbearer.

(1 Samuel 16:21 King James Bible)

So you will find favor and good repute In the sight of God and man.

(Proverbs 3:4 New American Standard Bible)

The angel said to her, "Do not be afraid, Mary; for you have found favor with God.

(Luke 1:30 New American Standard Bible)

8
Fear

Father in Heaven, I ask you to remove all fear and doubt from me as I serve in the name of Jesus, Amen.

ARMOR BEARER'S PRAYERS TO GOD

Powerful Scriptures
Armor Bearers and Servants of God can pray Daily

Fear

I am the one who comforts you, so why are you afraid of mere humans, who wither like the grass and disappear?

(Isaiah 51:12 NIV)

Be not afraid of them their faces, for I am with n you to deliver you, says the Lord.

(Jeremiah 1:8 Amplified Bible)

Do not tremble; do not be afraid! Did I not proclaim my purpose for you long ago? You are my witnesses- is there any other God? No! There is no other rock- not one!

(Isaiah 44:8NIV)

Fearing people is a dangerous trap, but trusting the lord means safety.

(Proverbs 29:25 NIV)

ARMOR BEARER'S PRAYERS TO GOD

Powerful Scriptures Armor Bearers and Servants of God can pray Daily

Fear

Do not be afraid of them; the Lord your God himself will fight for you.

(Deuteronomy 3:22 NIV)

The lord is my light and my salvation- who shall I fear? The Lord is the stronghold of my life- of who shall I be afraid?

(Psalms 27:1 NIV)

But you, dress yourself for work; arise, and say to them everything that I command you do not be dismayed by them, lest I dismay you before them.

(Jeremiah 1:17 NIV)

Fear is not of God. Rebuke it! For God has not given us a spirit of fear, but of power and of love and of a sound mind.

(2 Tim 1:7 NKJV)

ARMOR BEARER'S PRAYERS TO GOD

Powerful Scriptures Armor Bearers and Servants of God can pray Daily

Fear

And don't be afraid of the people, for I will be with you and will protect you. I the Lord have spoken.

(Jeremiah 1:8 New Living Translation)

For God has not given us a spirit of fear and timidity, but of power, love, and self-discipline.

(2 Timothy 1:7 NLT)

Serve only the Lord your God and fear him alone. Obey his commands, listen to his voice, and cling to him.

(Deuteronomy 13:4 NLT)

I am leaving you with a gift- peace of mind and heart. And the peace I give is a gift the world cannot give. So don't be troubled or afraid.

(John 14:27 NLT)

9

Forgiveness

Father in Heaven, help me to forgive those who hurt, mistreated, and used me in the name of Jesus, Amen.

ARMOR BEARER'S PRAYERS TO GOD

Powerful Scriptures
Armor Bearers and Servants of God
can pray Daily

Forgiveness

And be ye kind one to another, tenderhearted, forgiving one another, even as God for Christ's sake hath forgiven you

(Ephesians 4:32 KJV)

For if ye forgive men their trespasses, your heavenly Father will also forgive you

(Matthew 6:14-15 KJV)

Confess your faults one to another, and pray one for another, that ye may be healed. The effectual fervent prayer of a righteous man availeth much.

(James 5:16 KJV)

Forbearing one another, and forgiving one another, if any man have a quarrel against any: even as Christ forgave you, so also do ye.

(Colossians 3:13 KJV)

ARMOR BEARER'S PRAYERS TO GOD

Powerful Scriptures
Armor Bearers and Servants of God
can pray Daily

Forgiveness

Judge not, and ye shall not be judged: condemn not, and ye shall not be condemned: forgive, and ye shall be forgiven

(Luke 6:37 KJV)

"Blessed are those whose lawless deeds are forgiven, and whose sins are covered; blessed is the man against whom the Lord will not count his sin."

(Romans 4:7-8 English standard Version)

Then Jesus said to her, "Your sins are forgiven."

(Luke 7:48 NIV)

Then Peter came up and said to him, "Lord, how often will my brother sin against me, and I forgive him? As many as seven times?" Jesus said to him, "I do not say to you seven times, but seventy times seven.

(Matthew 18:21-22 ESV)

10

Fruits of the Spirit

Father in Heaven, I pray the Fruits of the Spirit will operate through me and make me Christ like as I serve for the Kingdom of God in the name of Jesus, Amen.

ARMOR BEARER'S PRAYERS TO GOD

Powerful Scriptures
Armor Bearers and Servants of God
can pray Daily

Fruits of the Spirit

But the fruit of the Spirit is love, joy, peace, forbearance, kindness, goodness, faithfulness, gentleness and self-control. Against such things there is no law.

(Galatians 5:22-23 NIV)

All discipline for the moment seems not to be joyful, but sorrowful; yet to those who have been trained by it, afterwards it yields the peaceful fruit of righteousness.

(Hebrews 12:11 New American Standard Bible)

And the seed whose fruit is righteousness is sown in peace by those who make peace.

(James 3:18 New American Standard Bible)

ARMOR BEARER'S PRAYERS TO GOD

Powerful Scriptures
Armor Bearers and Servants of God
can pray Daily

Fruits of the Spirit

But I say, walk by the Spirit, and you will not gratify the desires of the flesh7 For the desires of the flesh are against the Spirit, and the desires of the Spirit are against the flesh, for these are opposed to each other, to keep you from doing the things you want to do. But if you are led by the Spirit, you are not under the law. Now the works of the flesh are evident: sexual immorality, impurity, sensuality, idolatry, sorcery, enmity, strife, jealousy, fits of anger, rivalries, dissensions, divisions, envy, drunkenness, orgies, and things like these. I warn you, as I warned you before, that those who do such things will not inherit the kingdom of God.

(Galatians 5:16-21 English Standard Version)

11

God's Chosen

Father in Heaven, continue to use me as your chosen instrument, and let others see you in me as I serve your people in the name of Jesus, Amen.

Powerful Scriptures
Armor Bearers and Servants of God can pray Daily

God's Chosen

Therefore, as God's chosen people, holy and dearly loved, clothe yourselves with compassion, kindness, humility, gentleness and patience. Bear with each other and forgive one another if any of you has a grievance against someone. Forgive as the Lord forgave you. And over all these virtues put on love, which binds them all together in perfect unity. Let the peace of Christ rule in your hearts, since as members of one body you were called to peace. And be thankful.

(Colossians 3:12-15 NIV)

It is not that we think we are qualified to do anything on our own. Our qualification comes from God.

(2 Corinthians 3:5 New Living Translation)

As a prisoner for the Lord, then, I urge you to live a life worthy of the calling you have received. Be completely humble and gentle; be patient, bearing with one another in love. Make every effort to keep the unity of the Spirit through the bond of peace. There is one body and one Spirit, just as you were called to one hope when you were called; one Lord, one faith, one baptism; one God and Father of all, who is over all and through all and in all.

(Ephesians 4:1-6 NIV)

ARMOR BEARER'S PRAYERS TO GOD

Powerful Scriptures
Armor Bearers and Servants of God
can pray Daily

God's Chosen

And David came to Saul, and stood before him:
and he loved him greatly; and he became his armorbearer.

(1Samuel 16:21 ASV)

But now, thus says the LORD, your Creator, O Jacob,
And He who formed you, O Israel, "Do not fear, for I have redeemed you;
I have called you by name; you are Mine! "When you pass through the
waters, I will be with you; And through the rivers,
they will not overflow you When you walk through the fire, you will not
be scorched, Nor will the flame burn you.
"For I am the LORD your God, The Holy One of Israel, your Savior;
I have given Egypt as your ransom, Cush and Seba in your place.

(Isaiah 43:1-3 NAS)

12

Healed

*Father in Heaven, I ask you to heal me from past hurts,
so I can serve your people freely,
for your glory in Jesus name, Amen.*

Powerful Scriptures
Armor Bearers and Servants of God
can pray Daily

Healed

He sent his word, and healed them

Then they cry unto the LORD in their trouble, and he saveth them, and delivered them from their destructions.

(Psalms 107:20)

One of God's benefits is healing. Bless the LORD, O my soul; And all that is within me, bless His holy name. Bless the LORD, O my soul, And forget not all His benefits: Who forgives all your iniquities, Who heals all your diseases, Who redeems your life from destruction, Who crowns you with lovingkindness and tender mercies, Who satisfies your mouth with good things, So that your youth is renewed like the eagle's.

(Psalms 103:1-5 NKJV)

Choose to live. Be a fighter! "I call heaven and earth as witnesses today against you, that I have set before you life and death, blessing and cursing; therefore choose life, that both you and your descendants may live

(Deuteronomy 30:19 NKJV)

ARMOR BEARER'S PRAYERS TO GOD

Powerful Scriptures
Armor Bearers and Servants of God
can pray Daily

Healed

Believe, and you will receive. "Therefore I say to you, whatever things you ask when you pray, believe that you receive them, and you will have them.

(Mark 11:24 NKJV)

Plead your case to God. even I, am He who blots out your transgressions for My own sake; And I will not remember your sins. Put Me in remembrance; Let us contend together; State your case, that you may be acquitted.

(Isa 43:25-26 NKJV)

The devil wants to kill you; God wants to heal you. "The thief does not come except to steal, and to kill, and to destroy. I have come that they may have life, and that they may have it more abundantly.

(John 10:10 NKJV)

ARMOR BEARER'S PRAYERS TO GOD

Powerful Scriptures
Armor Bearers and Servants of God
can pray Daily

Healed

God's highest wish is for you to be well. Beloved, I wish above all things that thou mayest prosper and be in health, even as thy soul prospereth.

(3 John 1:2 KJV)

∞

Jesus has already paid the price for your healing. Who Himself bore our sins in His own body on the tree, that we, having died to sins, might live for righteousness; by whose stripes you were healed.

(1 Pet 2:24 NKJV)

∞

Be confident in your prayers. Now this is the confidence that we have in Him, that if we ask anything according to His will, He hears us. And if we know that He hears us, whatever we ask, we know that we have the petitions that we have asked of Him.

(1 John 5:14-15 NKJV)

∞

You can find strength in God and His Word". Let the weak say, "I am strong."

(Joel 3:10 NKJV)

13
Honor

*Father in Heaven, help me to honor you
in my serving others I pray in the name of Jesus, Amen.*

ARMOR BEARER'S PRAYERS TO GOD

Powerful Scriptures
Armor Bearers and Servants of God
can pray Daily

Honor

Children, obey your parents in the Lord, for this is right. "
Honor your father and mother,"
which is the first commandment with promise:
"that it may be well with you and you may live long on the earth.

(Ephesians 6:1-3 New King James Version (NKJV)

Be devoted to one another in love. Honor one another above yourselves.

(Romans 12:10 NIV)

In the same way, let your light shine before others,
that they may see your good deeds and glorify your Father in heaven.

(Matthew 5:6 NIV)

14
Jealousy

Father in Heaven, I ask you to remove all jealousy and envy away from me so others see your light radiating through me as I serve in the name of Jesus, Amen.

ARMOR BEARER'S PRAYERS TO GOD

Powerful Scriptures
Armor Bearers and Servants of God
can pray Daily

Jealousy

Let nothing be done through strife or vainglory;
but in lowliness of mind let each esteem other better than themselves.

(Philippians 2:3 KJV)

For ye are yet carnal: for whereas there is among you envying,
and strife, and divisions, are ye not carnal, and walk as men?

(1 Corinthians 3:3 KJV)

Set me as a seal upon thine heart, as a seal upon thine arm:
for love is strong as death; jealousy is cruel as the grave:
the coals thereof are coals of fire, which hath a most vehement flame.

(Song of Solomon 8:6 KJV)

For thou shalt worship no other god:
for the LORD, WHOSE NAME IS JEALOUS, IS A JEALOUS GOD

(Exodus 34:14 (KJV)

ARMOR BEARER'S PRAYERS TO GOD

Powerful Scriptures
Armor Bearers and Servants of God can pray Daily

Jealousy

Daniel in the Den of Lions (All of Chapter 6)

It pleased Darius to appoint 120 satraps to rule throughout the kingdom, with three administrators over them, one of whom was Daniel. The satraps were made accountable to them so that the king might not suffer loss. Now Daniel so distinguished himself among the administrators and the satraps by his exceptional qualities that the king planned to set him over the whole kingdom. At this, the administrators and the satraps tried to find grounds for charges against Daniel in his conduct of government affairs, but they were unable to do so. They could find no corruption in him, because he was trustworthy and neither corrupt nor negligent. Finally these men said, "We will never find any basis for charges against this man Daniel unless it has something to do with the law of his God."

So these administrators and satraps went as a group to the king and said: "May King Darius live forever! The royal administrators, prefects, satraps, advisers and governors have all agreed that the king should issue an edict and enforce the decree that anyone who prays to any god or human being during the next thirty days, except to you, Your Majesty, shall be thrown into the lions' den. Now, Your Majesty, issue the decree and put it in writing so that it cannot be altered—in accordance with the law of the Medes and Persians, which cannot be repealed." So King Darius put the decree in writing.

ARMOR BEARER'S PRAYERS TO GOD

Powerful Scriptures Armor Bearers and Servants of God can pray Daily

Jealousy

Daniel (Continued)

Now when Daniel learned that the decree had been published, he went home to his upstairs room where the windows opened toward Jerusalem. Three times a day he got down on his knees and prayed, giving thanks to his God, just as he had done before. Then these men went as a group and found Daniel praying and asking God for help. So they went to the king and spoke to him about his royal decree: "Did you not publish a decree that during the next thirty days anyone who prays to any god or human being except to you, Your Majesty, would be thrown into the lions' den?"

The king answered, "The decree stands—in accordance with the law of the Medes and Persians, which cannot be repealed."

Then they said to the king, "Daniel, who is one of the exiles from Judah, pays no attention to you, Your Majesty, or to the decree you put in writing. He still prays three times a day." When the king heard this, he was greatly distressed; he was determined to rescue Daniel and made every effort until sundown to save him.

ARMOR BEARER'S PRAYERS TO GOD

Powerful Scriptures Armor Bearers and Servants of God can pray Daily

Jealousy

Daniel (Continued)

Then the men went as a group to King Darius and said to him, "Remember, Your Majesty, that according to the law of the Medes and Persians no decree or edict that the king issues can be changed."

So the king gave the order, and they brought Daniel and threw him into the lions' den. The king said to Daniel, "May your God, whom you serve continually, rescue you!" A stone was brought and placed over the mouth of the den, and the king sealed it with his own signet ring and with the rings of his nobles, so that Daniel's situation might not be changed. Then the king returned to his palace and spent the night without eating and without any entertainment being brought to him. And he could not sleep.

At the first light of dawn, the king got up and hurried to the lions' den. When he came near the den, he called to Daniel in an anguished voice, "Daniel, servant of the living God, has your God, whom you serve continually, been able to rescue you from the lions?"

Daniel answered, "May the king live forever! My God sent his angel, and he shut the mouths of the lions. They have not hurt me, because I was found innocent in his sight. Nor have I ever done any wrong before you, Your Majesty."

ARMOR BEARER'S PRAYERS TO GOD

Powerful Scriptures Armor Bearers and Servants of God can pray Daily

Jealousy

Daniel (Continued)

The king was overjoyed and gave orders to lift Daniel out of the den. And when Daniel was lifted from the den, no wound was found on him, because he had trusted in his God.

At the king's command, the men who had falsely accused Daniel were brought in and thrown into the lions' den, along with their wives and children. And before they reached the floor of the den, the lions overpowered them and crushed all their bones.

Then King Darius wrote to all the nations and peoples of every language in all the earth:

"May you prosper greatly!

"I issue a decree that in every part of my kingdom people must fear and reverence the God of Daniel.

"For he is the living God and he endures forever;

ARMOR BEARER'S PRAYERS TO GOD

Powerful Scriptures
Armor Bearers and Servants of God
can pray Daily

Jealousy

Daniel (Continued)

his kingdom will not be destroyed,
his dominion will never end.
He rescues and he saves;
he performs signs and wonders
in the heavens and on the earth.
He has rescued Daniel
from the power of the lions."

So Daniel prospered during the reign of Darius
and the reign of Cyrus the Persian.

15
Judgment

*Father in Heaven, help me not to judge my leaders
or anyone else I pray in Jesus name, Amen.*

Powerful Scriptures
Armor Bearers and Servants of God can pray Daily

Judgment

Grudge not one against another, brethren, lest ye be condemned: behold, the judge standeth before the door. Take, my brethren, the prophets, who have spoken in the name of the Lord, for an example of suffering affliction, and of patience. Behold, we count them happy which endure. Ye have heard of the patience of Job, and have seen the end of the Lord; that the Lord is very pitiful, and of tender mercy. But above all things, my brethren, swear not, neither by heaven, neither by the earth, neither by any other oath: but let your yea be yea; and your nay, nay; lest ye fall into condemnation.

(James 5:9-12 KJV)

And this is the message I proclaim--that the day is coming when God, through Christ Jesus, will judge everyone's secret life.

(Romans 2:16 NIV)

Therefore judge nothing before the appointed time; wait until the Lord comes. He will bring to light what is hidden in darkness and will expose the motives of the heart. At that time each will receive their praise from God.

(1 Corinthians 4:5 NIV)

You, then, why do you judge your brother or sister? Or why do you treat them with contempt? For we will all stand before God's judgment seat.

(Romans 14:10 NIV)

ARMOR BEARER'S PRAYERS TO GOD

Powerful Scriptures Armor Bearers and Servants of God can pray Daily

Judgment

Judge not, that ye be not judged. For with what judgment ye judge, ye shall be judged: and with what measure ye mete, it shall be measured to you again.

(Matthew 7:1-2 KJV)

God *"will repay each person according to what they have done." To those who by persistence in doing good seek glory, honor and immortality, he will give eternal life. But for those who are self-seeking and who reject the truth and follow evil, there will be wrath and anger. There will be trouble and distress for every human being who does evil: first for the Jew, then for the Gentile; but glory, honor and peace for everyone who does good*

(Romans 2:6-10 NIV)

For by your words you will be justified, and by your words you will be condemned.

(Matthew 12:37 ESV)

Then the Lord knows how to rescue the godly from trials, and to keep the unrighteous under punishment until the day of judgment.

(2 Peter 2:9 ESV)

16
Listen

Father in Heaven, help me to listen to your instructions concerning the assignment you have called me too in the name of Jesus, Amen.

ARMOR BEARER'S PRAYERS TO GOD

Powerful Scriptures Armor Bearers and Servants of God can pray Daily

Listen

This is the confidence we have in approaching God: that if we ask anything according to his will, he hears us

(1 John 5:14 NIV)

Hearing and Doing the Word

Know this, my beloved brothers: let every person be quick to hear, s low to speak, slow to anger; for the anger of man does not produce the righteousness of God. Therefore put away all filthiness and rampant wickedness and receive with meekness the implanted word, which is able to save our souls.

But be doers of the word, and not hearers only, deceiving yourselves. For if anyone is a hearer of the word and not a doer, he is like a man who looks intently at his natural face in a mirror. For he looks at himself and goes away and at once forgets what he was like. But the one who looks into the perfect law, the law of liberty, and perseveres, being no hearer who forgets but a doer who acts, he will be blessed in his doing.

(James 1:19-25 ESV)

Powerful Scriptures
Armor Bearers and Servants of God
can pray Daily

Listen

My dear brothers and sisters, take note of this: Everyone should be quick to listen, slow to speak and slow to become angry.

(James 1:19 NIV)

Whatever you have learned or received or heard from me, or seen in me put it into practice. And the God of peace will be with you.

(Philippians 4:9 NIV)

What you have said in the dark will be heard in the daylight, and what you have whispered in the ear in the inner rooms will be proclaimed from the roofs.

(Luke 12:3 NIV)

But the face of the Lord is against those who do evil, to blot out their name from the earth.

(Psalms 34:16 NIV)

Whoever gives heed to instruction prospers, and blessed is the one who trusts in the Lord.

(Proverbs 16:20 NIV)

17

Love

Father in Heaven, help me to love others with a pure heart, and help me to love my enemies with the love of Christ in the name of Jesus, Amen.

Powerful Scriptures Armor Bearers and Servants of God can pray Daily

Love

If someone says, "I love God," and hates his brother, he is a liar; for he who does not love his brother whom he has seen, how can he love God whom he has not seen? And this commandment we have from Him: that he who loves God must love his brother also.

(1 John 4:20-21 NKJV)

And this is love: that we walk in obedience to his commands. As you have heard from the beginning, his command is that you walk in love.

(2 John 1:6 NIV)

Love does no harm to a neighbor. Therefore love is the fulfillment of the law.

(Romans 13:10 NIV)

Love must be sincere. Hate what is evil; cling to what is good. Be devoted to one another in love. Honor one another above yourselves. Never be lacking in zeal, but keep your spiritual fervor, serving the Lord. Be joyful in hope, patient in affliction, faithful in prayer. Share with the Lord's people who are in need. Practice hospital

(Romans 13:10 NIV)

ARMOR BEARER'S PRAYERS TO GOD

Powerful Scriptures Armor Bearers and Servants of God can pray Daily

Love

Bless those who persecute you; bless and do not curse. Rejoice with those who rejoice; mourn with those who mourn. Live in harmony with one another. Do not be proud, but be willing to associate with people of low position. Do not be conceited.

(Romans 12:14-16 NIV)

Do not repay anyone evil for evil. Be careful to do what is right in the eyes of everyone. If it is possible, as far as it depends on you, live at peace with everyone. Do not take revenge, my dear friends, but leave room for God's wrath, for it is written: "It is mine to avenge; I will repay, says the Lord." On the contrary

"If your enemy is hungry, feed him; if he is thirsty, give him something to drink". In doing this, you will heap burning coals on his head. Do not be overcome by evil, but overcome evil with good.

(Romans 12:17-21 NIV)

Do to others as you would have them do to you.

(Luke 6:31 NIV)

Powerful Scriptures
Armor Bearers and Servants of God
can pray Daily

Love

But love your enemies, do good to them,[1] and lend to them without expecting to get anything back. Then your reward will be great, and you will be sons[2] of the Most High,[3] because he is kind to the ungrateful and wicked

(Luke 6:35 NIV)

Love is patient,[1] love is kind. It does not envy, it does not boast, it is not proud. It is not rude, it is not self-seeking,[3] it is not easily angered,[4] it keeps no record of wrongs. Love does not delight in evil[6] but rejoices with the truth.[7] [5] It always protects, always trusts, always hopes, always perseveres.[8] Love never fails. But where there are prophecies,[9] they will cease; where there are tongues,[10] they will be stilled; where there is knowledge, it will pass away.

(1 Corinthians 13:4-8 NIV)

Hatred stirs up dissension, but love covers over all wrongs

(Proverbs 10:12 NIV)

I love you, O LORD, my strength.

[1](Psalm 18:1 NIV)

18
Lying

Father in Heaven, forgive me for the times I lied to my family members, friends and my leaders in the name of Jesus, Amen.

ARMOR BEARER'S PRAYERS TO GOD

Powerful Scriptures
Armor Bearers and Servants of God
can pray Daily

Lying

The LORD detests lying lips, but he delights in people who are trustworthy.

(Proverbs 12:22 NIV)

"For the mouth of the wicked and the mouth of the deceitful are opened against me: they have spoken against me with a lying tongue." They compassed me about also with words of hatred; and fought against me without a cause. For my love they are my adversaries: but I give myself unto prayer.

(Psalms 109:2-4 KJV)

"Do not steal." Do not deceive or cheat one another.

(Leviticus 19:11 New Living translation)

Don't lie to each other, for you have stripped off your old sinful nature and all its wicked deeds.

(Colossians 3:9 New Living Translation)

19
Mercy

Father in Heaven, I ask you to have mercy on me in the name of Jesus, Amen.

ARMOR BEARER'S PRAYERS TO GOD

Powerful Scriptures
Armor Bearers and Servants of God
can pray Daily

Mercy

Have mercy upon me, O God, according to thy lovingkindness: according unto the multitude of thy tender mercies blot out my transgressions. Wash me throughly from mine iniquity, and cleanse me from my sin.

For I acknowledge my transgressions: and my sin is ever before me.

Against thee, thee only, have I sinned, and done this evil in thy sight: that thou mightest be justified when thou speakest, and be clear when thou judgest.

Behold, I was shapen in iniquity; and in sin did my mother conceive me.

Behold, thou desirest truth in the inward parts: and in the hidden part thou shalt make me to know wisdom.

Purge me with hyssop, and I shall be clean: wash me, and I shall be whiter than snow.

Make me to hear joy and gladness; that the bones which thou hast broken may rejoice.

ARMOR BEARER'S PRAYERS TO GOD

Powerful Scriptures Armor Bearers and Servants of God can pray Daily

Mercy (Continued)

*Hide thy face from my sins,
and blot out all mine iniquities.*

*Create in me a clean heart, O God;
and renew a right spirit within me.*

*Cast me not away from thy presence;
and take not thy holy spirit from me.*

*Restore unto me the joy of thy salvation;
and uphold me with thy free spirit.*

*Then will I teach transgressors thy ways;
and sinners shall be converted unto thee.*

*Deliver me from bloodguiltiness,
O God, thou God of my salvation:
and my tongue shall sing aloud of thy righteousness.*

*O Lord, open thou my lips;
and my mouth shall shew forth thy praise.*

(Psalms 51:1-15 KJV)

ARMOR BEARER'S PRAYERS TO GOD

Powerful Scriptures
Armor Bearers and Servants of God
can pray Daily

Mercy (Continued)

For thou desirest not sacrifice; else would I give it:
thou delightest not in burnt offering.

The sacrifices of God are a broken spirit:
a broken and a contrite heart,
O God, thou wilt not despise.

Do good in thy good pleasure unto Zion:
build thou the walls of Jerusalem.

Then shalt thou be pleased with the sacrifices of righteousness,
with burnt offering and whole burnt offering:
then shall they offer bullocks upon thine altar.

(Psalms 51:16-19 KJV)

20
Obedience

*Father in Heaven, help me to obey every word you have given me concerning my assignment.
I pray, in Jesus name, Amen.*

ARMOR BEARER'S PRAYERS TO GOD

Powerful Scriptures
Armor Bearers and Servants of God
can pray Daily

Obedience

We demolish arguments and every pretension that sets itself up against the knowledge of God,[1] and we take captive every thought to make it obedient[2] to Christ.

(2 Corinthians 10:5 NIV)

Obey your leaders[1] and submit to their authority. They keep watch over you[2] as men who must give an account. Obey them so that their work will be a joy, not a burden, for that would be of no advantage to you.

(Hebrews 13:17 NIV)

He replied, "Blessed rather are those who hear the word of God[1] and obey it."

[2] **(Luke 11:28 NIV)**

his book of the law shall not depart out of thy mouth; but thou shalt meditate therein day and night, that thou mayest observe to do according to all that is written therein: for then thou shalt make thy way prosperous, and then thou shalt have good success.

(Joshua 1:8 KJV)

21
Patience

Father in Heaven, give me the patience I need to serve my leaders effectively in Jesus name, Amen.

ARMOR BEARER'S PRAYERS TO GOD

Powerful Scriptures
Armor Bearers and Servants of God
can pray Daily

Patience

I am not saying this because I am in need, for I have learned to be content whatever the circumstances. I know what it is to be in need, and I know what it is to have plenty. I have learned the secret of being content in any and every situation, whether well fed or hungry, whether living in plenty or in want. I can do all this through him who gives me strength

(Philippians 4:11-13 NIV)

A Psalm of David.

The LORD is my shepherd; I shall not want.

*He maketh me to lie down in green pastures:
he leadeth me beside the still waters.*

*He restoreth my soul: he leadeth me in the paths
of righteousness for his name's sake.*

*Yea, though I walk through the valley of the shadow of death,
I will fear no evil: for thou art with me;
thy rod and thy staff they comfort me.*

*Thou preparest a table before me in the presence of mine enemies:
thou anointest my head with oil; my cup runneth over.*

*Surely goodness and mercy shall follow me all the days of my life:
and I will dwell in the house of the LORD for ever.*

(Psalms chapter 23 KJV)

22
Protection

Father in Heaven, protect me from the enemies of this world in the name of Jesus, Amen.

ARMOR BEARER'S PRAYERS TO GOD

Powerful Scriptures Armor Bearers and Servants of God can pray Daily

Protection

Every word of God proves true. He is a shield to all who come to him for protection.

(Proverbs 30:5 New Living Translation)

The LORD keeps you from all harm and watches over your life.

(Psalms 121:7 New Living Translation)

God is our refuge and strength, A very present help in trouble.

(Psalms 46:1 New American Standard Version)

ARMOR BEARER'S PRAYERS TO GOD

Powerful Scriptures
Armor Bearers and Servants of God can pray Daily

Protection

Psalm 91

*Whoever dwells in the shelter of the Most High
will rest in the shadow of the Almighty I will say of the L*ORD*,
"He is my refuge and my fortress,
my God, in whom I trust."*

*Surely he will save you
from the fowler's snare
and from the deadly pestilence.
He will cover you with his feathers,
and under his wings you will find refuge;
his faithfulness will be your shield and rampart.
You will not fear the terror of night,
nor the arrow that flies by day,
nor the pestilence that stalks in the darkness,
nor the plague that destroys at midday.
A thousand may fall at your side,
ten thousand at your right hand,
but it will not come near you.
You will only observe with your eyes
and see the punishment of the wicked.*

ARMOR BEARER'S PRAYERS TO GOD

Powerful Scriptures
Armor Bearers and Servants of God can pray Daily

Protection

Psalm 91 (Continued)

*If you say, "The LORD is my refuge,"
and you make the Most High your dwelling,
no harm will overtake you,
no disaster will come near your tent.
For he will command his angels concerning you
to guard you in all your ways they will lift you up in their hands,
so that you will not strike your foot against a stone.
You will tread on the lion and the cobra; you will*

*But the Lord is faithful. He will establish you
and guard you against the evil one*

(2 Thessalonians 3:3 ESV)

ARMOR BEARER'S PRAYERS TO GOD

Powerful Scriptures
Armor Bearers and Servants of God can pray Daily

Protection

Psalm 91 (Continued)

trample the great lion and the serpent.

*"Because he loves me," says the L*ORD*, "I will rescue him;*
I will protect him, for he acknowledges my name.
He will call on me, and I will answer him;
I will be with him in trouble,
I will deliver him and honor him.
With long life I will satisfy him
and show him my salvation."

(Psalms 91 NIV)

No weapon that is fashioned against you shall succeed,
and you shall confute every tongue that rises against you in judgment.
This is the heritage of the servants of the Lord
and their vindication from me, declares the Lord."

(Isaiah 54:17 ESV)

23
Purpose

Father in Heaven, help me to fulfill my purpose here on earth as I continue to serve in ministry in the name of Jesus, Amen.

ARMOR BEARER'S PRAYERS TO GOD

Powerful Scriptures Armor Bearers and Servants of God can pray Daily

Purpose

"Agree with God, and be at peace; thereby good will come to you."

(Job 22:21 English Standard Version)

loved by God, that he has chosen you

(1 Thessalonians 1:4 NIV)

For we are his workmanship, created in Christ Jesus for good works, which God prepared beforehand, that we should walk in them.

(Ephesians 2:10 English Standard Version)

And the peace of God, which surpasses all understanding, will guard your hearts and your minds in Christ Jesus.

(Philippians 4:7 English Standard Version)

ARMOR BEARER'S PRAYERS TO GOD

Powerful Scriptures Armor Bearers and Servants of God can pray Daily

Purpose

But, as it is written, "What no eye has seen, nor ear heard, nor the heart of man imagined, what God has prepared for those who love him" these things God has revealed to us through the Spirit. For the Spirit searches everything, even the depths of God. For who knows a person's thoughts except the spirit of that person, which is in him? So also no one comprehends the thoughts of God except the Spirit of God. Now we have received not the spirit of the world, but the Spirit who is from God, that we might understand the things freely given us by God. And we impart this in words not taught by human wisdom but taught by the Spirit, interpreting spiritual truths to those who are spiritual.

(1 Corinthians 2:9-13 English Standard Version)

24
Righteous

Father in Heaven, control the way I think. Help me to think like you think and to keep my mind on you in the name of Jesus, Amen.

ARMOR BEARER'S PRAYERS TO GOD

Powerful Scriptures
Armor Bearers and Servants of God
can pray Daily

Righteous

*The eyes of the LORD watch over those who do right;
his ears are open to their cries for help.*
(Psalms 34:15 New Living Translation)

*Or ministry, let us wait on our ministering: or he that teacheth,
on teaching; Or he that exhorteth, on exhortation: he that giveth,
let him do it with simplicity; he that ruleth, with diligence;
he that sheweth mercy, with cheerfulness.
Let love be without dissimulation. Abhor that which is evil;
cleave to that which is good. Be kindly affectioned one to another
with brotherly love; in honour preferring one another;
Not slothful in business; fervent in spirit; serving the Lord;
Rejoicing in hope; patient in tribulation; continuing instant in prayer;
Distributing to the necessity of saints; given to hospitality.
Bless them which persecute you: bless, and curse not.
Rejoice with them that do rejoice, and weep with them that weep.
Be of the same mind one toward another. Mind not high things,
but condescend to men of low estate. Be not wise in your own conceits. Recompense to no man evil for evil. Provide things honest in the sight
of all men. If it be possible, as much as lieth in you,
live peaceably with all men. Dearly beloved, avenge not yourselves,
but rather give place unto wrath: for it is written, Vengeance is mine; I
will repay, saith the Lord. Therefore if thine enemy hunger, feed him;
if he thirst, give him drink: for in so doing thou shalt heap
coals of fire on his head. Be not overcome of evil,
but overcome evil with good.*

(Romans 12:7-21KJV)

25
Revenge

Father in Heaven, bless those who plot against me and desire to hurt me, and give me a spirit of discernment to know my enemies in the name of Jesus, Amen.

Powerful Scriptures
Armor Bearers and Servants of God can pray Daily

Revenge

Do not take revenge, my dear friends, but leave room for God's wrath, for it is written: "It is mine to avenge; I will repay," says the Lord.

(Romans 12:19 NIV)

Do not be overcome by evil, but overcome evil with good.

(Romans 12:21 NIV)

You shall not take vengeance, nor bear any grudge against the sons of your people, but you shall love your neighbor as yourself; I am the LORD.

(Leviticus 19:18 New American Standard Bible)

Do not say, "I will repay evil"; Wait for the LORD, and He will save you

(Proverbs 20:22 New American Standard Bible)

ARMOR BEARER'S PRAYERS TO GOD

Powerful Scriptures Armor Bearers and Servants of God can pray Daily

Revenge

"But I say to you who hear, love your enemies, do good to those who hate you, bless those who curse you, pray for those who mistreat you." Whoever hits you on the cheek, offer him the other also; and whoever takes away your coat, do not withhold your shirt from him either "Give to everyone who asks of you, and whoever takes away what is yours, do not demand it back. "Treat others the same way you want them to treat you." If you love those who love you, what credit is that to you? For even sinners love those who love them. "If you do good to those who do good to you, what credit is that to you? For even sinners do the same." If you lend to those from whom you expect to receive, what credit is that to you? Even sinners lend to sinners in order to receive back the same amount. "But love your enemies, and do good, and lend, expecting nothing in return; and your reward will be great, and you will be sons of the Most High; for He Himself is kind to ungrateful and evil men." Be merciful, just as your Father is merciful.

(Luke 6 27-36 NIV)

But Jesus was saying, "Father, forgive them; for they do not know what they are doing " And they cast lots, dividing up His garments among themselves.

(Luke 23:34 NIV)

26
Salvation

*Father in Heaven, I ask you to forgive me of all my sins.
I acknowledge and confess with my mouth that Jesus is Lord and
I believe in my heart that God raised Jesus from the dead,
and now I am saved in Jesus name, Amen.*

ARMOR BEARER'S PRAYERS TO GOD

Powerful Scriptures
Armor Bearers and Servants of God
can pray Daily

Salvation

However, I consider my life worth nothing to me; my only aim is to finish the race and complete the task the Lord Jesus has given me the task of testifying to the good news of God's grace.

(Acts 20:24 NIV)

The Lord is not slow in keeping his promise, as some understand slowness. Instead he is patient with you, not wanting anyone to perish, but everyone to come to repentance.

(2 Peter 3:9 NIV)

For this is what the Lord has commanded us: "I have made you a light for the Gentiles, that you may bring salvation to the ends of the earth."

(Acts 13:47 NIV)

Jesus looked at them and said, "With man this is impossible, but not with God; all things are possible with God."

(Mark 10:27 NIV)

27
Suffering

Father in Heaven, break generational curses from my life and my leader's life, I pray in the name of Jesus, Amen.

ARMOR BEARER'S PRAYERS TO GOD

Powerful Scriptures Armor Bearers and Servants of God can pray Daily

Suffering

Giving no offence in any thing, that the ministry be not blamed:

But in all things approving ourselves as the ministers of God, in much patience, in afflictions, in necessities, in distresses,

In stripes, in imprisonments, in tumults, in labours, in watchings, in fastings;

By pureness, by knowledge, by longsuffering, by kindness, by the Holy Ghost, by love unfeigned,

By the word of truth, by the power of God, by the armour of righteousness on the right hand and on the left,

By honour and dishonour, by evil report and good report: as deceivers, and yet true;

As unknown, and yet well known; as dying, and, behold, we live; as chastened, and not killed;

As sorrowful, yet alway rejoicing; as poor, yet making many rich; as having nothing, and yet possessing all things.

(2 Corinthians 6: 3-10)

Blessed is the one who perseveres under trial because, having stood the test, that person will receive the crown of life that the Lord has promised to those who love him.

(James 1:12 NIV)

ARMOR BEARER'S PRAYERS TO GOD

Powerful Scriptures
Armor Bearers and Servants of God
can pray Daily

Suffering

But He knows the way that I take He has concern for it, appreciates, and pays attention to it. When He has tried me, I shall come forth as refined gold [pure and luminous].

(Job 23:10 AMP)

Establishing and strengthening the souls and the hearts of the disciples, urging and warning and encouraging them to stand firm in the faith, and [telling them] that it is through many hardships and tribulations we must enter the kingdom of God.

(Acts 14:22 AMP)

I consider that our present sufferings are not worth comparing with the glory that will be revealed in us.

(Romans 8:18 NIV)

But even if you should suffer for what is right, you are blessed. "Do not fear their threats; do not be frightened."

(1 Peter 3:14 NIV)

ARMOR BEARER'S PRAYERS TO GOD

Powerful Scriptures Armor Bearers and Servants of God can pray Daily

Suffering

Carry each other's burdens, and in this way you will fulfill the law of Christ.

(Galatians 6:2 NIV)

Who shall separate us from the love of Christ? Shall trouble o r hardship or persecution or famine or nakedness or danger or sword?

(Romans 8:35 NIV)

Whoever does not take up their cross and follow me is not worthy of me.

(Matthew 10:38 NIV)

For it has been granted to you on behalf of Christ not only to believe in him, but also to suffer for him.

(Philippians 1:29 NIV)

28
Trouble

Father in Heaven, carry my burdens and place your easy yoke upon me in the name of Jesus, Amen.

ARMOR BEARER'S PRAYERS TO GOD

Powerful Scriptures
Armor Bearers and Servants of God
can pray Daily

Trouble

The righteous cry out, and the LORD hears them;
he delivers them from all their troubles.

(Psalms 34: 17 NIV)

The blessing of the LORD makes a person rich,
and he adds no sorrow with it.

(Proverbs 10:22 New Living Translation)

Then call on me when you are in trouble, and I will rescue you,
and you will give me glory." All praise to God,
the Father of our Lord Jesus Christ.
God is our merciful Father and the source of all comfort.

(Psalms 50:15 New Living Translation)

Of David. The LORD is my light and my salvation-- whom shall I fear?
The LORD is the stronghold of my life-- of whom shall I be afraid?

(Psalms 27:1 NIV)

ARMOR BEARER'S PRAYERS TO GOD

Powerful Scriptures
Armor Bearers and Servants of God
can pray Daily

Trouble

*For in the day of trouble he will keep me safe in his dwelling;
he will hide me in the shelter of his sacred tent
and set me high upon a rock.*

(Psalms 27:5 NIV)

*I will carry out great vengeance on them and punish them
in my wrath. Then they will know that I am the LORD,
when I take vengeance on them.*

(Psalms 25:17 NIV)

*Trouble and distress have come upon me,
but your commands give me delight.*

(Psalms 119:143 NIV)

*I have told you all this so that you may have peace in me.
Here on earth you will have many trials and sorrows.
But take heart, because I have overcome the world.*
(John 16:33 New Living Translation)

29

Trust

Father in Heaven, give me the faith I need so I can trust you concerning my assignment in the name of Jesus, Amen.

ARMOR BEARER'S PRAYERS TO GOD

Powerful Scriptures
Armor Bearers and Servants of God
can pray Daily

Trust

The lions may grow weak and hungry,
but those who seek the LORD lack no good thing.

(Psalms 34:10 NIV)

Trust in the Lord with all your heart
and lean not on your own understanding;
in all your ways submit to him,
and he will make your paths straight.

(Proverbs 3:5-6 NIV)

Commit to the Lord whatever you do,
and he will establish your plans.

(Proverbs 16:3 NIV)

In God, whose word I praise
in God I trust and am not afraid.
What can mere mortals do to me?

(Psalms 56:4 NIV)

30
Weakness

Heavenly Father, give me strength and energy to do the work you have called me to do in the name of Jesus, Amen.

ARMOR BEARER'S PRAYERS TO GOD

Powerful Scriptures Armor Bearers and Servants of God can pray Daily

Weakness

In the same way, the Spirit helps us in our weakness. We do not know what we ought to pray for, but the Spirit himself intercedes for us through wordless groans. And he who searches our hearts knows the mind of the Spirit, because the Spirit intercedes for God's people in accordance with the will of God.

And we know that in all things God works for the good of those who love him, who have been called according to his purpose. For those God foreknew he also predestined to be conformed to the image of his Son, that he might be the firstborn among many brothers and sisters. ³⁰ And those he predestined, he also called; those he called, he also justified; those he justified, he also glorified.

(Romans 8:26-30 NIV)

"Keep watching and praying that you may not enter into temptation; the spirit is willing, but the flesh is weak."

(Matthew 26:41 New American Standard Bible)

ARMOR BEARER'S PRAYERS TO GOD

Powerful Scriptures
Armor Bearers and Servants of God
can pray Daily

Weakness

Therefore I am well content with weaknesses, with insults, with distresses, with persecutions, with difficulties, for Christ's sake; for when I am weak, then I am strong.

(2 Corinthians 12:10 New American Standard Bible)

"Keep watching and praying that you may not come into temptation; the spirit is willing, but the flesh is weak."

(Mark 14:38 New American Standard Bible)

Now we who are strong ought to bear the weaknesses of those without strength and not just please ourselves.

(Romans 15:1 New American Standard Bible)

Therefore, strengthen the hands that are weak and the knees that are feeble

(Hebrews 12:12 New American Standard Bible)

ARMOR BEARER'S PRAYERS TO GOD

Powerful Scriptures
Armor Bearers and Servants of God can pray Daily

Weakness

Be on the alert, stand firm in the faith, act like men, be strong.

(1 Corinthians 16:13 New American Standard Bible)

But he must ask in faith without any doubting, for the one who doubts is like the surf of the sea, driven and tossed by the wind.

(James 1:6 New American Standard Bible)

*The Lord GOD has given Me the tongue of disciples,
That I may know how to sustain the weary one with a word
He awakens Me morning by morning, He awakens
My ear to listen as a disciple.*

(Isaiah 50:4 New American Standard Bible)

31
Wisdom

Father in Heaven, give me wisdom to serve my leaders, and help me to serve my leaders by the leading of the Holy Spirit in the name of Jesus, Amen.

ARMOR BEARER'S PRAYERS TO GOD

Powerful Scriptures
Armor Bearers and Servants of God
can pray Daily

Wisdom

*Listen, my son, to your father's instruction
and do not forsake your mother's teaching.*

(Proverbs 1:8 NIV)

༄

*Good planning and hard work lead to prosperity,
but hasty shortcuts lead to poverty.*

(Proverbs 21:5 New Living Translation)

༄

*Be very careful, then, how you live not as unwise but as wise,
making the most of every opportunity, because the days are evil.
Therefore do not be foolish, but understand what the Lord's will is.*

(Ephesians 5:15-17 NIV)

༄

*For where you have envy and selfish ambition,
there you find disorder and every evil practice.*

(James 3:16 NIV)

༄

*Be wise in the way you act toward outsiders; make the most of
every opportunity. Let your conversation be always full of grace,
seasoned with salt, so that you may know how to answer everyone.*

(Colossians 4:5-6 NIV)

ARMOR BEARER'S PRAYERS TO GOD

Powerful Scriptures Armor Bearers and Servants of God can pray Daily

Wisdom

Who is wise and understanding among you? Let them show it by their good life, by deeds done in the humility that comes from wisdom.

(James 3:13 NIV)

When pride comes, then comes disgrace, but with humility comes wisdom.

(Proverbs 11:2 NIV)

Even fools are thought wise if they keep silent, and discerning if they hold their tongues.

(Proverbs 17:28 NIV)

ARMOR BEARER'S PRAYERS TO GOD

Powerful Scriptures
Armor Bearers and Servants of God
can pray Daily

Wisdom

*Wisdom's instruction is to fear the Lord,
and humility comes before honor.*

(Proverbs 15:33 NIV)

*The one who gets wisdom loves life;
the one who cherishes understanding will soon prosper*

(Proverbs 19:8 NIV)

Therefore everyone who hears these words of mine and puts them into practice is like a wise man who built his house on the rock.

(Matthew 7:24 NIV)

More from Dr. Tavane Glass

Often times, servants of God desire to serve their spiritual leaders and become their armor bearers. However, they fail to realize they're not equipped to serve their leaders. It is God who calls and equips us to serve our leaders not man. Therefore, the pur pose for writing this book is to inform armor bearers and servants of God on how to serve their leaders better. This book will give personal assistants the appropriate tools they will need to be successful, productive, and effective armor bearers and servants of God. In addition, this book will be a blessing to the body of Christ for the glory of God.

ISBN: 9781498408561

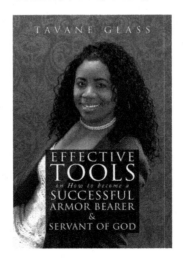

MORE FROM DR. TAVANE GLASS

The manual will teach, guide and assist armor bearers and personal assistants to become the best servants of God for the glory of God. Also, the manual will help simplify an armor bearer's day, and help personal assistants to be more organized as they serve their leaders. Therefore, it's purposeful for armor bearers and personal assistants to have this manual in their possession.

ISBN: 9781682730515

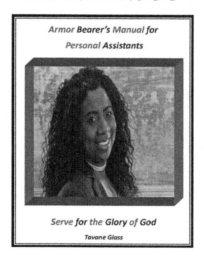

Author Contact:

www.tavaneglass.com

glass.tavane@gmail.com

TavaneGlass@facebook.com

TavaneGlass@twitter.com

TavaneGlass@instagram.com